LYNNFIELD PUBLIC LIBRARY

P9-CES-612

DATE DUE

LYNNFIELD PUBLIC LIBRARY
LYNNFIELD, MA 01940

TELLING TIME

HOW
to TELL TIME
on DIGITAL and
Analog Clocks!

ini Charlesbridge

written by

Jules Older

illustrated by

Megan Halsey

LYNNFIELD PUBLIC LIBRARY
LYNNFIELD, MA 01940

To 2:50 and 2:54 P.M., March 27, 1970
— J.O.

For 1:00 P.M., March 20th, 1999
— M.H.

The author and the illustrator are donating a portion of their royalties
for this book to Doctors Without Borders.

Text copyright © 2000 by Jules Older
Illustrations copyright © 2000 by Megan Halsey
All rights reserved, including the right of reproduction in whole or in part in any form.

Published by Charlesbridge Publishing
85 Main Street, Watertown, MA 02472
(617) 926-0329
www.charlesbridge.com

Library of Congress Cataloging-in-Publication Data
Older, Jules.
Telling Time / Jules Older ; illustrated by Megan Halsey.
p. cm. 4/7/00
Summary: Humorous text explains the concept of time, from seconds to hours
on both analog and digital clocks, from years to millennia on the calendar.
ISBN 0-88106-396-7 (reinforced for library use)
ISBN 0-88106-397-5 (softcover)
1. Time—Juvenile literature. [1. Time. 2. Clocks and watches.]
I. Halsey, Megan, ill. II. Title.
QB209.5.O38 2000
529'.7-dc21   99-18764

Printed in South Korea
(hc) 10 9 8 7 6 5 4 3 2 1
(sc) 10 9 8 7 6 5 4 3 2 1

The illustrations in this book were done in gouache paints and pen and ink on a fine Bristol paper.
The display type and text type were set in Tekton and Korinna.
Color separations were made by Sung In Printing Inc., South Korea
Printed and bound by Sung In Printing Inc., South Korea
Production supervision by Brian G. Walker
Designed by Megan Halsey

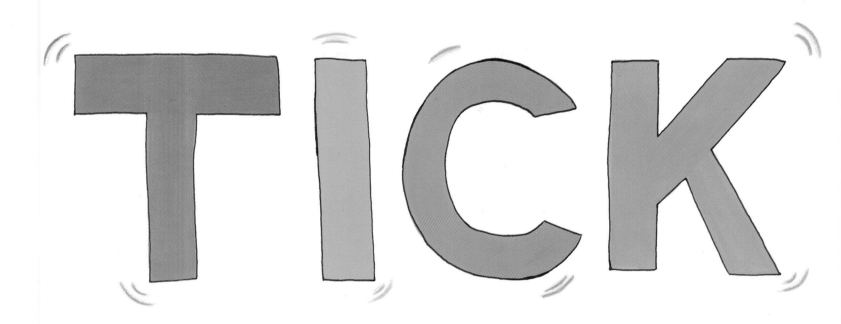

When people talk about telling time, they don't mean, "Hey, Time, I've got something to tell you!"

No, "telling time" just means saying what time it is.

And by the end of this book, you'll know how to tell what time it is!

But to learn how to tell time, shouldn't you know *what* time is?

Here's what time is. Time is: When things happen. And time is: How long things take.

When Things Happen

How Long Things Take

So that's what time is—**When Things Happen** and **How Long Things Take**.

OK, but *why* do we tell time? I'm so glad you asked.

We tell time so we'll know when school starts.

12:25

2:15

5:00

11:05

We tell time to know when our friends are coming over.

3:30

7:45

And if we couldn't tell time, we'd never see the beginning of a movie!

1:00

9:15

6:20

We tell time so we won't miss our favorite TV show.

4:50

10:35

8:35

That's why we tell time!

OK, OK, but *how* do we tell time?

We tell time in chunks.

Big chunks—**BIG, HUMUNGOUS CHUNKS**

and little chunks—eensy, itty-bitty chunklets. Shrimps.

Let's start with the shrimps. There are three kinds of little chunks.

The shortest little chunk is a **second**.

The middle-size little chunk is a **minute**. There are sixty seconds in every minute.

The longest little chunk is an **hour**.
There are sixty minutes in every hour.

"I had so much homework, it took me a whole hour to finish it!"

We tell the little chunks of time on clocks and watches.

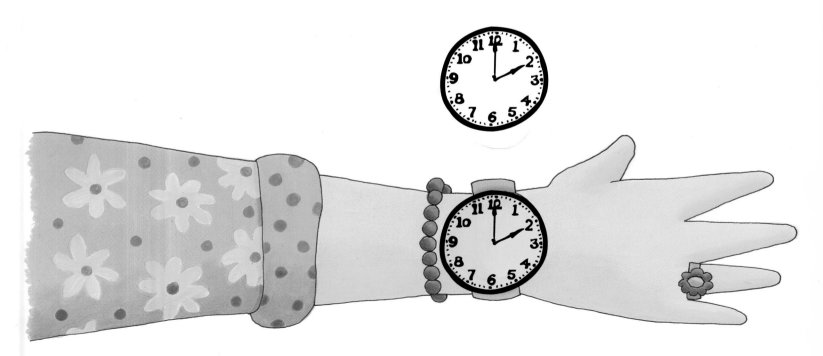

(A watch is just a clock you wear on your wrist.)

We tell the big chunks of time on calendars.

So what's a calendar?

It's that pretty picture with the numbers below it that hangs on the wall. And that stack of pages with numbers on them that sits on a desk.

A calendar tells the days. Every day has a name of its own:

Sunday,

Monday,

Tuesday,

Wednesday,

Thursday,

Friday, and

Saturday.

SUNDAY	MONDAY	TUESDAY	WEDNE
1	2 *first quarter moon*	3	
8	9	10 *full moo*	
15	16	17	
22	23	24	
29	30	31	

OCTO

DAY	THURSDAY	FRIDAY	SATURDAY
4	5	6	7
11	12	13	14
18	19 last quarter moon	20	21
25	26	27 new moon	28

BER

A calendar tells the months. Every month has a name of its own:
January,
February,
March,
April,
May,
June,
July,
August,
September,
October,
November, and
December.

A calendar tells the years:
1492, 1860, 1900,
1950, 2001, 2222.

And a calendar tells the dates:
Friday, October 1, 1999.
Saturday, January 1, 2000.
Monday, February 29, 2016.
(Do you know what's special about that date?)

2016 is a leap year.

What are the big chunks of time? Days, weeks, months, years—plus decades, centuries, and millennia.

The shortest big chunk is a **day**. You know what a day is.

Then comes a **week**. A week has seven days.

Then comes a **month**. A month has about thirty days and about four weeks.

SUN	MON	TUES	WED	THURS	FRI	SAT
OCTOBER 2000						
1	2	3	4	5 dentist ♡ 3:00	6	7 To Philadelphia
8 JEFF'S Birthday	9 BILL'S BIRTHDAY	10	11	12	13	14 Visit gramma & grampa
15	16 Robin here	17	18 lunch with Eleanor 12:00	19	20 6 month anniversary	21
22	23 to school with Melanie	24	25	26 Dr. Lipner 10:00	27	28 Jodi visits
29	30	31 Halloween				

Then comes a **year**. One year has 365 days. And it has almost exactly fifty-two weeks. And it has twelve months.

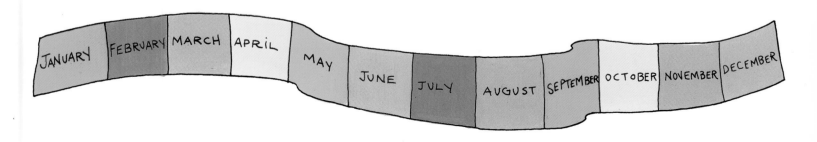

JANUARY FEBRUARY MARCH APRIL MAY JUNE JULY AUGUST SEPTEMBER OCTOBER NOVEMBER DECEMBER

Then comes a **decade**. A decade is ten years.

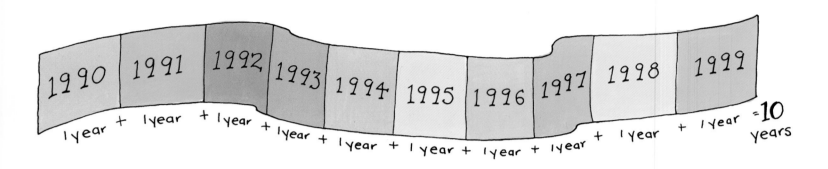

"Want to know how old I am? I'm a whole century old!"

The next biggest chunk is a **century**. A century lasts one hundred years.

The biggest chunk of time is a **millennium**. A millennium lasts a thousand years—ten centuries.

OK, OK, OK. Calendars show the big chunks: the days and months and all that. And clocks show the shrimps: seconds and minutes and hours and all that. But how do clocks show the seconds and minutes and hours? And all that?

Two ways—digital and analog.

A digital clock has big numbers in the middle. Here's a digital clock. . . .

An analog clock has little numbers around the edge and hands that point to the numbers. Here's an analog clock. . . .

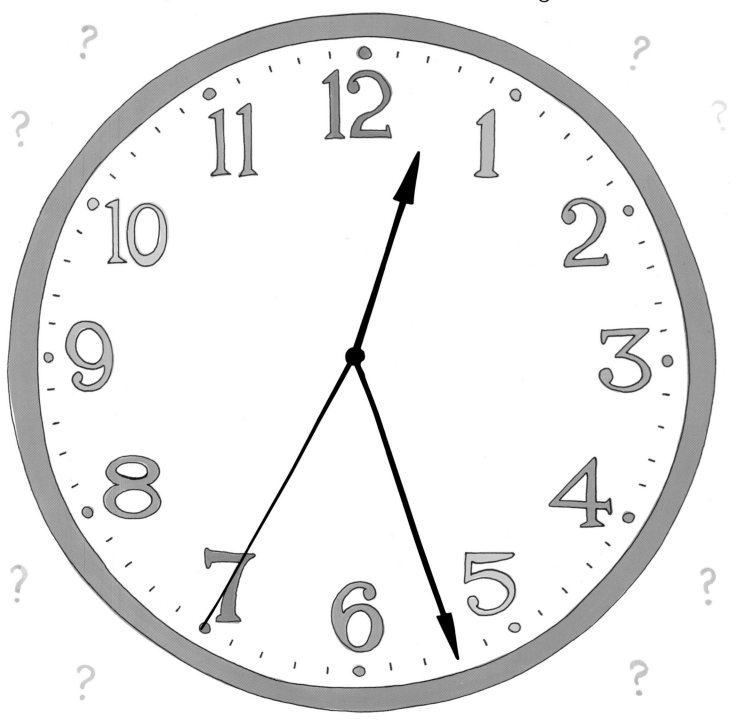

So, you want to learn how to tell time? Let's start with digital.
Digital clocks have two sets of numbers. One set comes before the colon sign (:) and the other comes after it.

The first numbers tell the hours. Look at this clock:

This number tells you it's three o'clock.

On this clock it says six o'clock.

On this one it says ten o'clock.

On this one it says twelve o'clock.

(Most clocks only go up to twelve o'clock, though there are twenty-four-hour clocks, too. There's no such thing as thirty-three o'clock. Or 127 o'clock.)

The numbers after the : mark the minutes. How many minutes are there in an hour? Sixty. Sixty minutes in an hour.

So 3:15 is fifteen minutes past three o'clock. Some people call that three-fifteen. Some call it quarter past three. They both mean the same thing.

This one is twenty-one minutes past six o'clock.

This one is forty-four minutes past ten o'clock. You can call it ten-forty-four. They both mean the same thing.

What does this clock say?

Some people call that twelve-thirty. Some call it half past twelve. They both mean the same thing.

How about this one?

That's ten minutes after one o'clock. Or one-ten. They both mean the same thing.

And this one?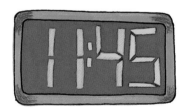

Some people call that eleven-forty-five. Some call it quarter of twelve. All together, now—**They both mean the same thing!**

So now you've got your minutes and your hours. One more thing: A.M. and P.M. When you are doing something in the morning, like eating breakfast, that's A.M. But if it's after noon—after twelve o'clock—like eating supper, that's P.M. So breakfast is at six A.M., but supper is at six P.M.

Now let's look at analog clocks, the ones with hands.
They're not really hands, not like people hands.
They don't have fingers; they don't wear mittens.
So why are they called hands? Because they point.
Like hands. Like this:

Clocks have three kinds of hands:

Little hands,

BIG hands,

and second hands.

Second hands tell the seconds.

Big hands tell the minutes.

Little hands tell the . . . the . . . want to guess?

Little hands tell the hours.

Those Funny-Looking Numbers

Some clocks have numbers that look a little strange. Those are Roman numbers.
They are called that because the Romans used them. Here's what they mean.

1 one	= I	5 five	= V	9 nine	= IX
2 two	= II	6 six	= VI	10 ten	= X
3 three	= III	7 seven	= VII	11 eleven	= XI
4 four	= IV	8 eight	= VIII	12 twelve	= XII

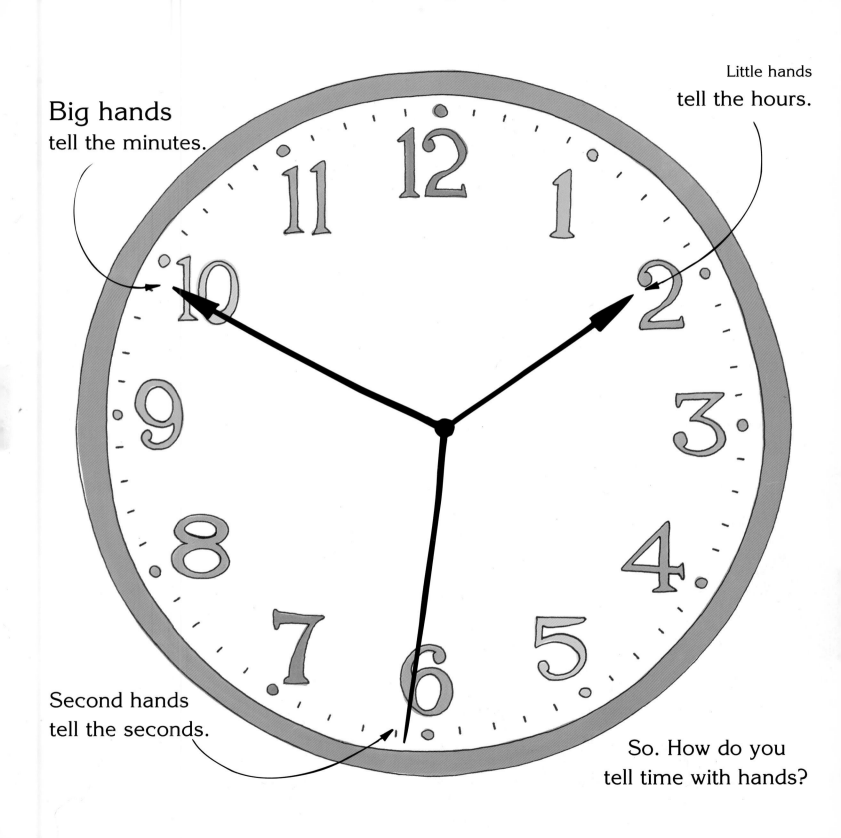

Big hands
tell the minutes.

Little hands
tell the hours.

Second hands
tell the seconds.

So. How do you
tell time with hands?

The second hand is easy. You can watch it move.
Every time it passes a number, that's another five seconds.
"You held your breath for 53 seconds. You're turning blue!"
Every time it passes the 12, up at the top of the clock,
that's a minute. Sixty seconds make one minute.

The **big minute hand**
moves slower than the second hand.
Every time it passes a number, that's
another five minutes. "Hurry up!
The movie starts in five minutes!"

It takes sixty minutes to go all
the way around. Sixty minutes
make one hour.

The little hour hand is the
slowest hand of all.

It takes one hour to go
between numbers. "Mom, I'm
starving! It's been one whole
hour since breakfast." It takes
twelve hours (!) to go all the
way around the clock.

So that's how to tell how long things take on an analog clock. But how do you tell **what time it is?** Look and see where the hands are! When the little hand is on the 3 and the big hand is on the 12, it's three o'clock.

How about when the little hand is on the 4?

How about when the little hand is on the 7?

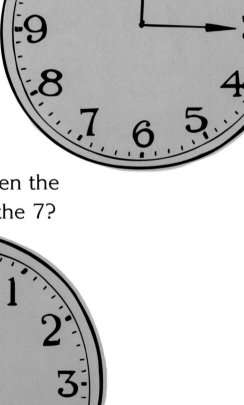

Right, it's four o'clock!

Yes! It's seven o'clock.
Here's a smiley face for you!

Now let's move the **big minute hand**, too. When the little hand is on the 3 and the **big hand** is on the 1, it's five minutes past three o'clock. Or you can call it three-o-five.

How about when the hour hand is halfway between the 7 and the 8 and the **minute hand** is on the 6?

Yes! It's seven-thirty. You deserve another smiley face!

OK, here's a tough one. What time is it when the little hand is almost on the 9 and the **big hand** is exactly on the 9?

The correct answer is . . . fifteen minutes to nine. Or eight-forty-five. Or quarter of nine.

And here's one that's even tougher. The little hand is just past the 9 and the **big hand** is only one dot past the 3. (Here's a hint. Remember, there are five minutes between each number. So if the 3 is fifteen minutes, one dot past the 3 is . . .)

Yes! The time is nine-sixteen.

Here are some more analog clocks.
See if you can tell the time. . . .

Great! Hey, guess what?
Now you're telling time!

Here's how to remember how big each chunk of time is:

sixty seconds make a minute

sixty minutes make an hour

twenty-four hours make a day

seven days make a week

four weeks or a little more make a month

twelve months make a year

ten years make a decade

ten decades make a century

ten centuries make a millennium.

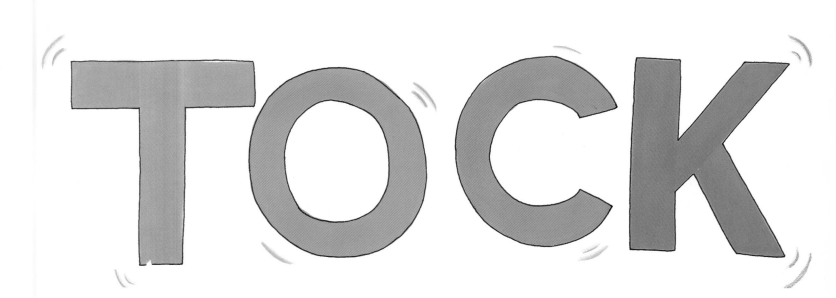

Here's a little poem to help you remember
how long things take. . . .

Sixty seconds make a minute,
That's a lot of seconds, innit?

Sixty minutes make an hour,
Long enough to take a shower.

Twenty-four hours in a day,
Just how long I want to play.

Seven days make one whole week,
10,080 minutes—eek!

A month is four weeks, sometimes more,
I'd like to spend it at the shore.

It takes twelve months to make a year,
When New Year's comes, we'll give a cheer!

Ten whole years a decade makes,
I'd love to eat ten decade cakes.

A century takes a long, long time,
One full year plus ninety-nine.

A thousand years is one millennium.
Write me a letter if you can think of
even one word that rhymes with millennium!

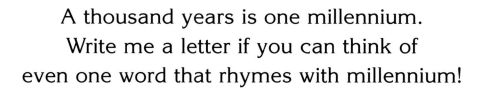

You now know how to tell the time,
So it's time to end this little rhyme.
And this little book, too.

THE  END

WWW Resources for Children

Brain, Marshall. "How Time Works." BYG Publishing, Inc. *http://www.howstuffworks.com/time.htm* (1998).
- Find out why there are sixty seconds in a minute and twenty-four hours in a day, learn what AM and PM mean, and discover why telling time is so important.

HiLink Communications. "Local Times around the World." *http://www.hilink.com.au/times/*
- Choose a place around the globe and find out if people there are eating breakfast or going to bed. Practice reading the digital clocks.

Savetz, Kevin. "Foam Bath Fish Time." *http://www.savetz.com/fishtime/?-4*.
- Practice reading a digital clock with these playful bath toys. Ask the fish to tell you what time it is anywhere in the world.

WWW Resources for Parents and Teachers

National Institute of Standards and Technology. "A Walk through Time" *http://physics.nist.gov/GenInt/Time/time.html* (Aug. 1997).
- Provides a history of telling time, a resource list, and much more.

Usher, Gordon T. "Clocks and Time." *http://www.ubr.com/clocks/index.html* (1997).
- Displays the official U.S. Naval Observatory time in digital format, provides historical information, and answers frequently asked questions about time.

* At the time of publication, all WWW addresses were correct and operational.

LYNNFIELD PUBLIC LIBRARY
LYNNFIELD, MA 01940